Life

JOURNEYS

DAILY READINGS: JEFF LUCAS
GROUP DISCUSSION QUESTIONS:
JEFF LUCAS AND ANDY PECK

CWR Applying God's Word
to everyday life and relationships

Copyright © CWR 2008
Published 2008 by CWR, Waverley Abbey House,
Waverley Lane, Farnham, Surrey GU9 8EP, UK.
Registered Charity No. 294387. Registered Limited
Company No. 1990308. Reprinted 2008.
Bible reading notes included in this booklet previously
published by CWR in the September/October 2006
issue of *Lucas on Life Every Day*, by Jeff Lucas.
The right of Jeff Lucas to be identified as the author
of this work has been asserted by him in accordance
with the Copyright, Designs and Patents Act 1988,
sections 77 and 78.
Questions for group discussion: Jeff Lucas and
Andy Peck.
All rights reserved. No part of this publication
may be reproduced, stored in a retrieval system, or
transmitted, in any form or by any means, electronic,
mechanical, photocopying, recording or otherwise,
without the prior permission in writing of CWR.
For a list of our National Distributors visit
www.cwr.org.uk/distributors
Unless otherwise indicated, all Scripture references
are from the Holy Bible: New International
Version (NIV), copyright © 1973, 1978, 1984 by the
International Bible Society.
Concept development, editing, design and production
by CWR
Printed in England by Nuffield Press Ltd.
ISBN: 978-1-85345-467-7

CONTENTS

INTRODUCTION

ELIJAH. His name means, 'The Lord is God' and, at first glance, it seems that the man always lived with the same certainty as his name. Elijah conquered his fears – most of the time. Here was a man who took on the most powerful, wicked, determined people ever, who pointed the prophetic finger at kings and queens, who learned to fear neither silence nor the impossible – nor even death itself. He was determined to go public with his faith, whatever the personal cost. But his case history is not without blemish. He also buckled under pressure, ignored the God who was passing by, and refused to put God's radical plans fully into action.

Sometimes I've heard great warriors described as people who are fearless. I'm not so sure that it's a helpful description. Surely even the bravest are not without fear – rather they refuse to be conquered by it, and have learned to push through and overcome, despite the huge wave of fear that threatens to overwhelm them at any moment.

Elijah went through seasons crippled by self-doubt, having lost all perspective, when his only prayer was for death itself. In short, his name sometimes meant 'The Lord is God?' – with an emphasis on the question mark. In other words, this lion heart was weak and flawed – just like us.

So let's look at the story of a fellow traveller who touched a nation – and be encouraged. We're called to live edgy, provocative lives that will challenge the status quo. Elijah has been there; his story can help us.

How to use

This resource is designed to include all you will need for four small-group sessions. It comprises four DVD clips, group discussion questions based on each clip and Bible readings to be used between each session.

PREPARATION

1. Watch the DVD clip before the meeting.

2. Use the icebreaker to get folk chatting. Select the questions that you think would be most useful for your group to look at. You may want to use them all, depending on the time you have available. We suggest you plan for 30–45 minutes.

THE SESSION

1. Play the DVD clip first and go straight into the icebreaker question.

2. Use the questions you have selected.

3. Move from discussion into prayer. There's a prayer included in the material which you could finish with at the end.

4. Encourage the group to use the daily readings in the days between sessions. The readings expand and build on the topics covered in the DVD. If the group members are not used to daily Bible reading, encourage them to develop this habit. If the group members are already into a routine of Bible reading and prayer each day you might want to discuss how best to work these new readings into their time.

5. You could start the next session by reviewing how the group found the daily readings. What did they learn? Do they have questions to raise? How did God speak?

Session 1:
Going Public, Being Brave

ICEBREAKER:
If it were illegal to be a Christian and you were convicted, would there be friends, colleagues or acquaintances who would be surprised?

FOR GROUP DISCUSSION:

• How do people typically understand the word 'Christian' in Britain today? How can you explain your own understanding so that people grasp what you mean by the word?

• How can we speak up for God in our nation without sounding like ranting fundamentalists – and what should we speak up about?

• What does it mean to 'live prophetically'?

• A sense of identity is vital – what does the Bible say about who we are in Christ?

- Christians in the UK are not persecuted as in many countries, but they may face discrimination. Have you ever experienced this? In what ways might Christians be discriminated against?

- What does it mean to 'invest in the invisible'?

- It is said that courage is simply not letting your fear prevent you from doing what is right. Can you think of a time when you were 'courageous'? How about a time when you 'wimped out'?

PRAYER:
Lord, You call us to courageous love.
Help us to speak for You, with clarity, with compassion,
and with lives that back up our words.
Grant us bravery,
and help us to remember who we are in Christ:
that we stand, not only before great challenges,
but before the One who can help us to live prophetic lives
that will serve as salt and light to our nation
– and to our world.
Amen.

PRAYER is not just a religious duty, something Christians do to prove that they are Christian. Prayer puts us before a living God who still speaks. It's a heart-racing, awesome experience to catch a sense that the God who created the universe is talking to *you*. Christians often speak of those times when a particular scripture seems to come alive with meaning, when God makes His eternal word a 'now' word.

Many people abuse the concept of God speaking, justifying everything they do – especially their bizarre and sometimes thoughtless actions – by announcing that 'God told me'. I have heard that phrase enough times to put me off the possibility that God might whisper something in my ear for the rest of my life.

But I'm quite wrong to react like that. The essence of Christianity is relationship; God is still in the business of conversation.

Surely that was the key to Elijah's praying. His request for a divinely commanded drought was not some idea that had popped into his head. As a man who knew the law, he knew that God decreed that idolatry would usher in a drought of judgment. His was biblically-inspired logic: Scripture had come alive in his heart, and now he felt confident to ask for what God had promised. He also knew that this would be a slap in the face for Baal, who was supposed to be 'The rider in the clouds', and the sender of rain. When the rains stopped, Baal-worshippers believed that their god was dead. This drought would send a clear message about who was in charge.

Feed on God's Word today. He still speaks.

Prayer: Bring Your Word to life in my heart, Lord. Speak: I am listening. Amen.

The word coming alive

BIG PICTURE:
James 5:17–18
Deuteronomy 11:13–17

FOCUS:
'He prayed earnestly that it would not rain, and it did not rain on the land for three and a half years.' (James 5:17)

God is still in the business of conversation

Clearing up confusion

BIG PICTURE:
1 Kings 17:1
Romans 1:8–16

FOCUS:
Elijah ... said to Ahab,
'As the LORD, the God
of Israel, lives, whom
I serve, there will be
neither dew nor rain in
the next few years except
at my word.'
(1 Kings 17:1)

WE SAW yesterday that a drought would send a clear signal to the worshippers of Baal – no rain, no god. But there was just one problem: their religion taught them that if Baal was dead, it would be at the hands of yet another god – and legend had it that the assassin was Mot, the god of death.

If drought came, Elijah knew that there was a possibility that Israel, from Ahab and Jezebel down, would turn once more to Yahweh. But what if, in their deluded dullness, they just switched allegiance to Mot instead? All of Elijah's prayerful work would be wasted. There was nothing else for it: someone would have to march into that threatening palace and tell them what was what. So Elijah had to take his life in his hands and stand before the fearsome royal couple. He knew that he might get a sword through the heart for his trouble.

In a culture where uncertainty is fashionable, we are called to live clearly for God. Political correctness has gone mad; that means we can feel that it is almost blasphemous to make any absolute truth claims about Jesus in a multi-faith, relativist society. But we are called to be loyal to our God, not the shifting trends of a confused culture. That doesn't excuse Christians who confuse rudeness and ranting for clarity, but still we are called to live – and speak – in such a way that leaves no one in any doubt as to where our loyalties lie.

Elijah calmly stood his ground. God help us do the same.

Prayer: Father, give me clarity untainted by arrogance, boldness to speak, mingled with a willingness to listen. Amen.

HOW on earth do you become brave?

I've often wondered how I'd perform if my faith were put to the test. Around the world today, our brothers and sisters in the persecuted Church are suffering because of their love and loyalty for Jesus Christ – there are more Christian martyrs now than there have ever been in Christian history. So, faced with pain or even death, would I quickly deny my faith and scurry away, branding myself forever as a weak coward – or would I be courageous?

Truthfully, I have no idea, and don't even bother to torment myself with the question anymore, seeing as I will only have God's strength and grace for that event if it actually happens. My speculation would be a waste of time. But as I ponder Elijah's standing before the might of Ahab's dark power, fully aware that a snap of the fingers from the king could mean a quick death – or worse, long, agonising torture – I wonder, how do you become that brave?

Perhaps there's a key in Elijah's prophetic language. He describes the God of Israel as the One he serves – a better translation is 'the One before I stand'. So Elijah stands before two kings – not one; however great Ahab's power was, Elijah was aware that the king of Israel was a tiny potentate compared with the might and majesty of his God.

Perhaps we're standing before an intimidating edifice of a problem today, and we feel small in its shadow and powerless before it. Look again: you also stand before a God who is bigger than all.

Prayer: Keep me conscious that I stand, Lord, before two powers: the challenges I face and You, my forever strong God. Amen.

Before two kings

BIG PICTURE:
**1 Kings 17:1
1 Corinthians
16:13–14**

FOCUS:
'As the LORD, the God of Israel, lives, whom I serve, there will be neither dew nor rain in the next few years except at my word.'
(1 Kings 17:1b)

... you also stand before a God who is bigger than all

Leaving it to God

BIG PICTURE:
**1 Kings 17:2–5
2 Chronicles 20:1–12**

FOCUS:
'Then the word of the
LORD came to Elijah:
"Leave here .. ." So he did
what the LORD had told
him.' (1 Kings 17:2a,5a)

I DON'T like those movies with ambiguous endings, where you don't know the final outcome. Having invested a couple of hours in watching it, I'd like to know what happened at the finish.

Elijah dropped his prophetic stun grenade in the palace and walked out – off the stage of Israel's national life for a whole year as God shunted him away to the brook Kerith. Without waiting for Ahab's response to his message, Elijah's off to enforced obscurity.

At first glance, it looks like Elijah did a proverbial 'runner' – rushing into hiding from what was now probably a seething king. But others too were in hiding; the senior civil servant Obadiah was running a secret refuge for prophets. So if Elijah wanted to hole up for a while, he could have joined them, where the benefits of community would have been his.

Consider as well that when Jezebel later issued a death threat to Elijah, he took matters in his own hands, ran away and hid, and God sent him straight back into that dangerous situation (1 Kings 19:3,15). Whatever the ultimate motivation here, it seems that at this earlier stage of Elijah's ministry, fear wasn't the dominating force that drove him – obedience was.

Obedience is the heart of discipleship. Sometimes, we don't feel like doing what is right, have a host of better ideas and wonder about the logic of doing things God's way. But obedience must be our daily choice.

Let's gladly submit to Him today: ultimately, it's for our own good.

Prayer: Thank You for Your rule and reign of love, not suppression. I gladly yield to You, Father. Amen.

JAMIE Oliver I'm not. So because I'm no culinary genius, my discovery of instant porridge has been a delight. Now, in just one hundred and twenty seconds, I can whip myself up a delicious concoction of oats with a hint of apples and blackberries. There is but one problem. Just lately, the two-minute wait has seemed so very long. I find myself cheering the microwave on, urging it to cook ever faster, desperate to hear that little chime that announces that my Scottish cuisine is ready for consumption. I like things fast.

I'd like to be a good Christian by this time tomorrow, praying with razor-sharp sensitivity and faith-packed authority. But most of all, I'd like to weigh in as a heavyweight when it comes to godly character: a significantly holy super-saint. Okay, it's not going to happen overnight. How about by Thursday afternoon?

But character is created in a slow cooker. Look at those verses again. Elijah didn't spend his days in a paradise location; Kerith was an ugly place, a gash in the desert. The weather was hot – often one hundred and twenty degrees in the afternoon – and the water would have been coated in thick, green algae. This was no crystal clear mountain stream. But he didn't just go there – he stayed there.

'God's man or woman', says Kierkegaard, 'is early selected and slowly educated for a job.' Kosuke Koyama writes in *Three Mile an Hour God*[1] that God works at the speed a person walks. Perhaps, like me, you find yourself where you don't want to be, painfully learning a long-term lesson in God's lifelong academy.

Be patient. God is.

Prayer: Lord, I long for the fruit of the Spirit – but forget that fruit takes time to grow. Give me patience with myself – and others. Amen.

Microwavable maturity

BIG PICTURE:
**1 Kings 17:1–6
2 Peter 3:18**

FOCUS:
'He went to the Kerith Ravine, east of the Jordan, and stayed there.' (1 Kings 17:5b)

Character is created in a slow cooker

1. Kosuke Koyama, *Three Mile an Hour God* (Maryknoll: Orbis books, 1980)

Session 2:
Living in the Real World

ICEBREAKER:
Get several daily 'broadsheet' newspapers and select stories that describe the way you would define 'the real world', as you see it.

FOR GROUP DISCUSSION:
- What do you do when life doesn't make sense?

- Has your care for someone ever left you feeling that you wished you hadn't bothered? How did you react?

- What's the difference between faith and trust?

- How do you feel when you're falsely accused, as Elijah was?

- When you think of home, which words come to mind? Are they always 'pleasant' words? How would your closest family or friends describe you – if they were really honest?

• What is the place of mystery in the life of faith?

• 'Kindness can change the world' – have you seen that in your life?

PRAYER:
Father,
help us to have trust
as well as faith,
kindness as well as authority,
and grace towards those who are closest to us.
Help us to respond rather than react
when we are falsely accused.
May we know
that miracles and mystery
sit together in Your purposes.
Amen.

Living with contradictions

FOCUS:
"'As surely as the LORD your God lives,' she replied, 'I don't have any bread .... I am gathering a few sticks to take home and make a meal ... that we may eat it – and die.'"
(1 Kings 17:12)

I LIKE it when life makes sense, God gives me guidance that is entirely logical, and my questions are answered. When I can understand, faith is an easier walk. Unfortunately, life often doesn't unfold that way, even if you are right in the centre of God's purposes for your life, as Elijah was at this moment.

Put yourself in his sandals. You're tired, hungry, and somewhat bewildered at the thought of showing up at a stranger's house for your first 'normal' meal in a year. You're looking forward to some conversation after months of isolation. But your host is a very confused, undernourished soul on the brink of death. When you ask her for something to eat, she declares that the cupboard is empty of food – and her heart void of hope. This is her last meal for her and her son, and then they would die. But God had promised provision from this poor woman's hands, and so another miracle unfolds.

Have you ever been in a situation when you sensed that God was asking something of you, and then circumstances seemed to pile up, one after the other, to contradict totally what you thought God had said? When that happens, *do* check, with trusted friends and prayerful counsel, that you have heard rightly. Terrible and sometimes tragic things have been done by Christians who insisted that they had heard from God – when it was wishful thinking that turned sour. But if God has spoken and you've taken responsible steps to check with Scripture and other mature Christians, then stand your ground, and don't be afraid.

Prayer: Father, help me trust that Your hand is at work, when circumstances suggest that You are nowhere to be found. Amen.

I AM currently feeling really quite spiritual. These last few days, prayer has been easier than usual, I've been able to think things through with an abnormal clarity, I sense I am hearing from God and, as far as I know, I've not irritated anyone for a while. You've guessed it – I'm alone, on a ten-day writing retreat. After an initial period of adjustment, where I had to get used to my own company, I quite like the solitude – at least for a while.

It's easier to be godly when alone. Walking and praying on the lush green South Downs in the South of England, as I've been able to do today, isn't demanding. Trying to love God and other humans when you are awakened by your children's violin practice at 7am (and you fear that a number of animals are being strangled) is not quite so easy. The test of our faith has to be in the hubbub of relationships.

In public, I can fake kindness. But around those nearest and dearest to me, I am the real me. American politician Mark Hatfield confesses: 'The home is the toughest environment of all for leaders. Why is it that the ones we love the most are the ones we are most impatient with? My wife has often said to me, "I wish you were as patient with your children as you are with your constituents."'

Elijah takes his place in a family home – where fresh challenges will come. Zarephath means 'smelting furnace' – and home and relationships will be the refining fire that shows what we *really* are.

Prayer: Give me faith for the silent times, faith when it is peaceful, when it is busy and when I'm surrounded by noise. Amen.

Home matters

BIG PICTURE:
1 Kings 17:13–16
Ephesians 5:1–6:4

FOCUS:
'So there was food every day for Elijah and for the woman and her family.'
(1 Kings 17:15b)

It's easier to
be godly
when alone

Rejection comes

BIG PICTURE:
1 Kings 17:17–18
Proverbs 15:1

FOCUS:
'She said to Elijah, "What do you have against me, man of God? Did you come to remind me of my sin and kill my son?"' (1 Kings 17:18)

WE SAW yesterday that it's in our own relationships that much of the refining work of God comes. One of the most difficult trials to walk through is when we are hurt by the very people we are closest to. If someone distant takes a swipe at me, it smarts, but I'm not mortally wounded. But if a close friend or family member disappoints, then the pain can be excruciating.

Elijah had walked through an ongoing daily miracle with the woman and her son, but when her boy dies, she turns on Elijah and strikes like a rattlesnake. Suddenly, it's Elijah's fault that the boy died (he would have died of starvation months earlier had it not been for the prophet), he has something against the woman (yes, that's why he prayerfully laid on a miracle for her) and he only came to remind her of her sin (now what sin would that be exactly, since no one has mentioned it until now?).

So what turned a happy home into a boxing ring? Notice how quickly the distraught woman links her son's death, Elijah's being in the home and her past sin together. There's a skeleton in the closet and it's making her angry and spiteful.

And so she hits out. Unresolved issues in our relationship with God will affect our relationships with others. When someone is unkind, stop and wonder what might be going on beneath the surface. Who knows what pain lingers behind those acid words? Perhaps the problem is not really with us at all. And how should we react? We'll consider that tomorrow.

Prayer: Help me to see past the surface when others hurt me: give me sensitivity to their pain, and the grace to respond well. Amen.

IT'S hard to meet contempt with kindness. It takes real grace to keep serving someone even as they attack you. Who knows, they might interpret your willingness to be gracious as an admission of guilt for the very things that they accuse you of. Now, they insist, you are trying to work off your shame! But Elijah is broken-hearted at the tragedy that has befallen this little family: there's no time for defensive words, or theological discussion about past sin – it is time to pray. We are clearly taught to pray for our enemies and for those who mistreat us. While the woman was not Elijah's enemy, she was acting like one. Surely we are changed as we pray for those who are unkind to us: we see them differently, and feel differently about them.

Elijah opens the floodgates of his heart with his praying – we get a glimpse of that 'praying in prayer' again as he rages at God. And in the unusual act of 'stretching' himself upon the boy three times, as he presses his body against the prone, cold body of that lad, some commentators suggest that he was taking a radical stance: 'my life for his life, let my breath be given for him.' Of course, in praying like this, Elijah touched a corpse – and that would make him ceremonially unclean for seven days (Num. 19:11).

As I contemplate Elijah praying like this, I confess my poverty in this area – I know very little about this kind of intensity and passion in intercession. Perhaps you'd like to join me as I ask God: Lord, teach us how to pray.

Prayer: Teach us to pray with passion, persistence, and love, even for those who bruise us with their words and deeds. Amen.

Kindness expressed through prayer

BIG PICTURE:
1 Kings 17:19–23
Luke 6:27–36

FOCUS:
'Then he cried out to the LORD, "O LORD my God, have you brought tragedy also upon this widow...?"'
(1 Kings 17:20a)

Lord, teach us
how to pray

Influence is ours

BIG PICTURE:
1 Kings 17:24
Matthew 5:13–16

FOCUS:
'Then the woman said to Elijah, "Now I know that you are a man of God and that the word of the LORD from your mouth is the truth."'
(1 Kings 17:24)

IMAGINE the atmosphere in that room as Elijah carried the once dead, now living son downstairs to a tearful reunion with his mother. But something more than physical resurrection has taken place here. When Elijah first showed up at this house, the woman spoke to him about the Lord *his* God (1 Kings 17:12). But now both she and her son have seen and experienced enough of the power and love of God, and she exclaims, 'the word of the LORD from your mouth is the truth.' She has come to see the reality about God for herself – and all because God choreographed things so that she would provide a lonely prophet with a home for a while.

It must have been impossible to live with a man like Elijah without bumping into God. I'm reminded of the story of Gordon Maxwell, who went to India as a missionary. So obvious was his faith and his behaviour, that when he asked a local Hindu to teach him the language, the man refused, claiming that if he spent time with Maxwell, he would inevitably become a Christian.

That's something to aspire to, especially as many of us quietly feel that living with us might have the opposite effect. Elijah lived the message in the home, before he took the next mighty step ... to the hill: onto the platform of confrontation at Mount Carmel.

Prayer: May those closest to me be drawn closer to You, through me. Amen.

Elijah lived the message in the home, before he took the next mighty step ...

Session 3:
The Clash of Convictions

ICEBREAKER:
Brainstorm the biggest threats to Christian witness in the UK. Vote on which the group thinks is the biggest. Is there anything you could/should do?

FOR GROUP DISCUSSION
• Have we reacted against 'cringy' evangelism so much that we now shy away from any forms of evangelism at all?

• What does it mean to make a stand for God?

• Have you experienced name-calling and insults for being a follower of Jesus? What was your reaction?

• How do we make good choices daily?

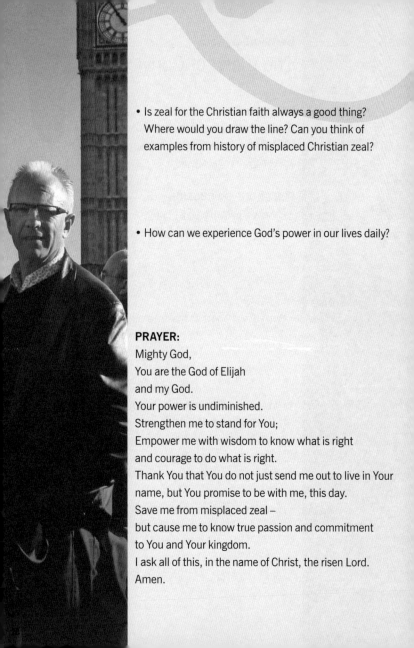

- Is zeal for the Christian faith always a good thing? Where would you draw the line? Can you think of examples from history of misplaced Christian zeal?

- How can we experience God's power in our lives daily?

PRAYER:
Mighty God,
You are the God of Elijah
and my God.
Your power is undiminished.
Strengthen me to stand for You;
Empower me with wisdom to know what is right
and courage to do what is right.
Thank You that You do not just send me out to live in Your name, but You promise to be with me, this day.
Save me from misplaced zeal –
but cause me to know true passion and commitment
to You and Your kingdom.
I ask all of this, in the name of Christ, the risen Lord.
Amen.

I'VE recently discovered another rather bizarre weakness in my life – one among many. I tend to agree with my critics immediately, rather than thinking through their criticisms. When told that I have done something wrong, I often apologise: which, at first glance seems quite noble. But is it? It's not always very honest (if I haven't done what I'm accused of, and I know it) and it is also linked with a basic desire to please people. If we're not sure that we're guilty of wrong, we'd be better to thank our accusers, and take some time to think and pray about their comments, rather than rushing to hold up our hands in surrender and falsely admit to something, just for the sake of peace.

As Elijah met Ahab, the surly king hurled an abusive, accusatory missile at the prophet, and denounced him as the 'troubler of Israel' – the Hebrew word here is a very strong insult, meaning 'one who brings disaster'. Ahab was convinced that his statement was true – this wasn't just royal name-calling. After all, Elijah had made it clear that it was by *his* word that drought would begin – and end. In a sense, Elijah was the choreographer of judgment. But a moment of reflection – and Elijah's blunt response – shows us that Ahab was also quite wrong, for judgment day had come because of *his* wickedness. Without hesitation, Elijah set the record straight. And the apostle Paul set the record straight too about his wrongful imprisonment. Be open and humble when someone suggests that you got it wrong – listen, take advice, and be prayerful. But don't plead guilty when you're not.

Prayer: Lord, help me put things right when I'm wrong, but save me from confessing to what I have not done. Amen.

Wrongly accused

BIG PICTURE:
**1 Kings 18:16–18
Acts 16:16–40**

FOCUS:
"'I have not made trouble for Israel,' Elijah replied. "But you and your father's family have. You have abandoned the LORD's commands and have followed the Baals.'" (1 Kings 18:18)

... don't plead guilty when you're not

You can't have it both ways

BIG PICTURE:
1 Kings 18:18–21
Joshua 24:1–15

FOCUS:
'How long will you waver
between two opinions? If
the Lord is God, follow
him; but if Baal is God,
follow him.'
(1 Kings 18:21)

THE Christian life is often compared to running in a race; images of sleek athletes striding down the track come to mind, unless you're me. I run every day, and the word stagger is more appropriate to describe my style of running. At times, an oxygen tent from above would be helpful as I limp my way through the last torturous yards.

In challenging the gathered people of Israel, Elijah uses a term (translated 'waver' here) that means 'to limp'. They have wavered backwards and forwards between Yahweh and Baal, perhaps trying to get the best of both religions. Baal was primarily a weather-god and handy at harvest time. Yahweh, on the other hand, may have been popularly thought of as a god from the desert regions of Sinai (see Hab. 3:3–7). Some thought of Yahweh as 'a god of the hills and not a god of the valleys' (1 Kings 20:28). Baalism certainly came in useful if you wanted some sexual indulgence: you could sin away and still feel spiritual.

Now the people have to make a choice – it's one or the other. You and I face that choice daily: the tempter doesn't usually throw down the gauntlet and demand that we totally abandon our love for God – but subtly invites us to mix up a cocktail, a little compromise here, a dash of self-indulgence there. Perhaps, at the beginning of another day, it would be good to set our sights on decisive living, where we follow God – wholeheartedly. Limping isn't fun; it's painful, looks terrible, and ultimately will slow your jogging down to a complete stop. Let's choose well.

Prayer: Father, give me grace to say 'Yes' to You, and 'No' to that which draws me away from You. Amen.

WE SAW yesterday that 'limping' Christianity will characterise our experience if we fail to be decisive about our choices. But sometimes, like Israel on Mount Carmel, we don't openly refuse God – we just stay in silent rebellion, lips sealed, arms folded.

In Herman Melville's *Bartleby the Scrivener*, Bartleby is a scribe who copies legal documents. The meek and mild Bartleby is liked and appreciated by his employer, but then the boring and previously predictable clerk begins to rebel. Asked to proofread a document, Bartleby refuses, and uses a phrase that becomes the theme of the rest of the book: 'I'd prefer not to.' Soon every request from the employer, no matter how reasonable, is met with the same wooden response: 'I'd prefer not to.' The employer, who could have simply fired Bartleby, desperately and yet patiently tries to win him over and coax him with kindness; but eventually, Bartleby refuses to do any work, and incredibly, makes the office his permanent home, establishing squatter's rights. Once again the employer embodies longsuffering and kindness, and invites Bartleby to vacate the office building and live in his home; amazing grace that is met by the same reply: 'I'd prefer not to.'

Ultimately, selfish Bartleby is hauled off to jail, where he goes on hunger strike. His former employer visits him, pleading with him to take some food: 'I'd prefer not to.' As the book ends, the narrator, pondering the polite but unyielding Bartleby, exclaims, 'Ah, Bartleby! Ah, humanity!'

Silence sometimes isn't golden – just solid rebellion. Are there areas where we're smiling at heaven – but saying, 'I'd prefer not to'?

Prayer: When You speak Lord, I will listen – and answer. Amen.

I'd prefer not to

BIG PICTURE:
1 Kings 18:20–21
Jeremiah 13:1–11

FOCUS:
'But the people said nothing.'
(1 Kings 18:21b)

Are there areas where we're smiling at heaven – but saying, 'I'd prefer not to'?

Desperate dancing

BIG PICTURE:
1 Kings 18:22–29
Ephesians 2:1–10

FOCUS:
'Elijah began to taunt them. "Shout louder! ... Surely he is a god! Perhaps he is deep in thought, or busy, or travelling. Maybe he is sleeping and must be awakened."'
(1 Kings 18:27)

THE prophets of Baal moved into a frenzied, six-hour religious workout, desperate to provoke a fiery response from the heavens. The word that is used to describe their dancing is the same word that we considered a couple of days ago – the one that means 'staggering'.

With his provocative sense of humour, Elijah hovers in the background, making comments about the need to wake Baal up – an inside joke, as Baal was believed to be a vegetation deity who had to be awakened each spring from his winter hibernation. Most modern translators have cleaned up Elijah's other little joke, about Baal 'going travelling' – a term that probably means 'gone aside to relieve oneself'.

But freeze the frame for a moment, and consider these desperate dancers: everything is based on them making their god do something. If they can just leap high enough, scream loud enough, or even spill enough of their own blood (as they resort to cutting themselves) then perhaps their deity will torch their sacrifice. This same notion of the 'pay as you pray' god was behind the unspeakable evil of child sacrifice: blessing, if it was coming, would have to be purchased. Human nature rushes to adopt that spiritual equation. There's no such thing as a free lunch, or for that matter, a free pardon. Whatever I get, I'll settle the bill.

Today, there's nothing we can do to make God love us more, and nothing we can do to make God love us less. Salvation really is the ultimate free gift, the greatest present in history.

Prayer: Thank You, Father, for giving me what I could never earn. Help me to pass on news of that gift. Amen.

IT'S one of those terrible scenes that occur in Old Testament history, as the prophets of Baal are executed without delay – or trial. Commentators are divided: some insist that Elijah was just fulfilling the law (Deut. 13:1–5) in ordering the executions. And remember the countless babies that had suffered an agonising death at the hands of these evil occultists.

But others wonder if Elijah went a step too far – as we've noted, there was no trial (perhaps the evidence was plain) but the day does end with what seems like a lynching, the mob ruling, even though the mob was under the command of Elijah. One commentator suggests that Elijah had a tendency towards fanaticism. As we'll see in the next few days, the man of miracles certainly didn't always get it right, and occasionally his perception was completely wrong.

Perhaps we should simply heed the warning never to allow passionate faith to become damaging fanaticism. Someone once said 'A fanatic is just someone who is more committed to God than you are' – but though that sounds challenging and noble, it's not helpful. A fanatic is not just someone who flies an aeroplane into a building in the name of their god; they go to extremes to demonstrate their commitment, insisting that everyone 'does faith' their way. They go beyond the demands of God, placing extra rules upon themselves or others. The Corinthians went too far in their discipline of one of their number. Fanaticism can be difficult to judge in others, though, so let's be careful to look out for it in ourselves and reluctant to judge it in others.

Prayer: Lord, show me how to walk in the balance and rhythm of grace. Amen.

Faithful – or fanatical?

BIG PICTURE:
1 Kings 18:30–40
2 Corinthians 2:1–11

FOCUS:
'Elijah commanded them, "Seize the prophets of Baal. Don't let anyone get away!" They seized them, and Elijah had them brought down to the Kishon Valley and slaughtered there. (1 Kings 18:40)

never ... allow

passionate faith

to become

damaging

fanaticism

Session 4:
Prophet at a Loss

ICEBREAKER:
Get some paper and pens and ask the group to draw
pictures/symbols representing their fears. (The pictures
don't have to be masterpieces!)

FOR GROUP DISCUSSION
- Have you ever been close to 'stress' or 'burnout'? (Stress
  can be seen as weariness from events or activities you
  didn't enjoy; burnout, as exhaustion from something you
  did enjoy.)

- What did you do?

- Depression is a liar. How does it lie?

- Typically, what drains you emotionally?

- Are there areas of your life where you have lost hope for
  change?

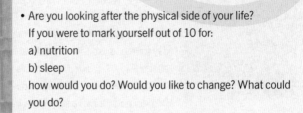

- Are you looking after the physical side of your life?
  If you were to mark yourself out of 10 for:
  a) nutrition
  b) sleep
  how would you do? Would you like to change? What could
  you do?

- Are you doing what God has told you to do?

PRAYER:
Save me from fear,
loving God,
as I affirm again
that my life is in Your hands.
Help me to see through the lies
that sadness can tell me,
and help me to live in and by Your truth.
Fill me with hope.
Amen.

The power of fear

BIG PICTURE:
1 Kings 19:1–3
Psalm 27:1–14

FOCUS:
'Jezebel sent a messenger to Elijah to say, "May the gods deal with me ... if by this time tomorrow I do not make your life like that of one of them."'
(1 Kings 19:2)

I CAN remember spending a whole summer under the cudgel of fear. I'd heard through the grapevine that a large, muscle-bound lad in our neighbourhood was out to get me. He had a terrifying reputation, having put a few other people in hospital, and I awoke every day with the same suffocating dread. Perhaps today would be the day for me to experience hospital food. After six weeks of agonising, I decided to go to his workplace to see if the rumours were true. We met, and he treated me like an old friend: I had thrown a summer away, sacrificed to fear.

It was fear that toppled Elijah. Jezebel was a devilishly clever strategist – she could have had Elijah killed, just as other prophets of God had died at her command. But in the wake of the Carmel contest, that wouldn't have been politically expedient. It could provoke a national uprising if the new hero from Gilead was suddenly executed. She realised that she didn't have to kill him – just tell him that she was planning to do so, and let fear do its devastating, gnawing work in his mind and soul.

Her message is loaded with intimidation: one translation of her words is 'I am Jezebel. You are Elijah'. She reminds him of her royal power, and of his humble background.

Perhaps we're more vulnerable after an emotional and spiritual high. Now the man who had looked Ahab in the eye, who hadn't flinched at a fight with a herd of prophets of Baal, buckles as the messenger departs. The smart weapon of fear had scored a hit, right on target.

Prayer: Father, my imagination can summon many threats. Quieten my heart, and help me trust You when I am afraid. Amen.

IN Colorado, where I live, we have a few bears wandering around in the woods – and once in a while, down the high street of our town. In bygone days, a bear trap was used (thankfully, it's illegal now) that slammed shut and locked onto the foot of the bear. It was particularly cruel: the more the animal struggled, the more terrible damage was done.

Making things worse

BIG PICTURE:
1 Kings 19:4–5
Luke 22:49–51

FOCUS:
'... while he himself went a day's journey into the desert. He came to a broom tree, sat down under it and prayed that he might die.'
(1 Kings 19:4)

Elijah is struggling like a man caught in a trap – and only hurting himself more. One of the results of our reacting rather than responding to crisis, and insisting that we go it alone, is that we end up either working hard but changing nothing or, in some cases, making things worse than they already are. By running as he did, Elijah stayed well in the danger zone, because he fled to Judah, forgetting that Ahab's daughter was reigning there with Jehoram (2 Kings 8:16–18). He travelled more than eighty miles – for nothing.

If that weren't pointless enough, notice that he ran for his life – and then prayed for death – a somewhat illogical course of action. Moses had prayed this prayer at a time of great discouragement (Num. 11:15), and so had Jonah (Jonah 4:3).

And then, probably already exhausted by the tumultuous events on Mount Carmel, he makes things worse because of the physical demands of the journey, which was 'too much for him'. Burned out, he loses all perspective – about who he was called to be, and what God had done. If you feel trapped today – be careful about action that could make things worse. Don't run like Elijah, or strike out like Peter, who panicked in the Garden of Gethsemane.

Prayer: Lord, steady my nerve when I am under pressure. Let my choices reflect faith, not fear. Amen.

If you feel trapped today – be careful about action that could make things worse

Exhausted

BIG PICTURE:
1 Kings 19:5–9a
John 21:1–14

FOCUS:
'The angel of the LORD came back a second time and touched him and said, "Get up and eat, for the journey is too much for you."' (1 Kings 19:7)

I AM rather nervous of those spiritual Christians who don't ever seem to have down days. Perhaps I'm just envious, but although I occasionally camp out in a place called victory, I can't say that I live there. And when I'm tired, or jet lagged, I've noticed that my capacity to believe in God is sharply diminished. Give me enough sleep deprivation, and I can identify easily with my friend Adrian Plass, who says that there are times when he is an Olympic-level doubter.

Helpfully, God knows and is concerned about these practical details. So the angel of the Lord showed up, not with a thousand friends to tap dance on the clouds and hum the hallelujah chorus, or even to give the worn-out prophet a blinding revelation – but to cook him breakfast, and help him rest. Just like Jesus really: it was an unusual priority for Him, having beaten death and hell, to show up on a beach and cook breakfast for His worn-out disciples – but the fact that He did gives us a glimpse of how utterly marvellous He is.

Sometimes a good breakfast is exactly what we need. God knows that there are moments when what we need is not another ministry assignment, prayer meeting, or Bible study – but a hot meal and a good sleep. I've met too many Christians who will immediately decide that they are under serious spiritual attack, when they don't need to lock horns with the devil but take a nap.

Let's be spiritual and sensible, and endeavour to take care of our work, rest and play: He is interested in all of it.

Prayer: Give me wisdom to establish rhythm in my life Lord. And thank You that You sometimes bless – through breakfast. Amen.

FORGET the idea that God only leads His children into safe places. Elijah was called to operate in a strategy that appeared to be suicidal. The Aramites were the enemies of Israel – so why would Elijah anoint a foreign king? They were being called to bring judgment upon Israel – and remove Ahab and Jezebel.

But it got worse. Now Elijah was being told to anoint another king over Israel itself, in readiness to take over – Jehu, a man who would have a heart for revival, and who would ultimately deal with Jezebel. But to anoint another king would send the already-incensed Jezebel into a fit of rage. Then the issue of succession for Elijah was dealt with, in the command to anoint Elisha.

So did Elijah obey? Yes and no. He *did* anoint Elisha. He *didn't* anoint Hazael – Elisha had to do that later. And he didn't anoint Jehu. When Ahab's reign ended, Jehu wasn't waiting in the wings. Ahaziah, Ahab's son, reigned two years, and he was just like his father. Then there was Jehoram, another son of Ahab, who was just a little better, but not much, and his reign was inconsequential. Thirteen years were wasted – and then Elisha, now at the helm, anointed another king – Jehu – the man picked out years earlier!

Jehu wasn't perfect, and drifted back into apostasy, but he stamped out the worship of Baal by tricking the god's followers into meeting together and then slaughtering them, also destroying their temple (2 Kings 10:18–28).

Even if God's command is costly, and indeed risky, do what He says. To disobey is to waste precious time.

Prayer: Lord, help me to obey You when I don't understand, and when what You call me to looks precarious. Amen.

A radical plan

BIG PICTURE:
1 Kings 19:9–18
Isaiah 55:8–13

FOCUS:
'The LORD said to him, "Go back the way you came, and go to the Desert of Damascus. When you get there, anoint Hazael king over Aram."' (1 Kings 19:15)

To disobey

is to waste

precious time

After Sinai: Elisha

BIG PICTURE:
1 Kings 19:19–21
Psalm 145:1–21

FOCUS:
'Elisha ... took his yoke of oxen and slaughtered them. He burned the plowing equipment to cook the meat and gave it to the people ... Then he set out to follow Elijah ...'
(1 Kings 19:21)

... the call to disciple is a command, not an option

TODAY I heard of the death of a dear man who, years ago spent hours with me when I was a brand-new Christian. He was a minister who had been struck down by multiple sclerosis. Housebound, and unable to function in church leadership, he refused to waste his life, but instead poured his failing energy into young Christians like me. He never mocked my questions, or rejected me when I failed. I will be forever grateful for him.

Elijah's influence faded after Sinai – perhaps because he didn't follow through on the instructions that he had received there. In a period of between ten and fifteen years, he only ministered twice publicly, as well as sending a prophetic word through the postal system. These were turbulent years, but years when Elijah was mostly silent. But he did raise up and invest in a worthy successor.

At a recent conference I heard Jim Partridge, a young man who has a passion to see the young people of Britain reached for Jesus. Jim called for a Church that is 'filled with youth workers', where we don't just rely upon the youth leader or full-time youth worker for the discipleship of their young people, but where everybody takes responsibility to be one generation telling the story of God to another.

Investing in others takes time and patience. We will be disappointed by some drifting away – especially some of those that showed great promise. We will need to answer endless questions that seem obvious, allow our busy schedules to be interrupted. But the call to disciple is a command, not an option.

Prayer: Lord, grant me grace not only to look for blessing, but to become a blessing, and leave a legacy. Amen.

Lucas on Life Every Day

If you've enjoyed this DVD, why not apply the Scriptures to your life with Jeff's daily Bible reading notes?

His mix of passion, humour and practical insight will enable you to live the Christian life successfully in the twenty-first century.

ISSN: 1774-0122
£2.49 each (plus p&p) published bimonthly
£13.80 (plus p&p) UK annual subscription (six issues)

Other Life Journey DVDs in the series:

Friends Rediscovered –
Learn how to form friendships that will endure and become richer with passing years.
EAN: 5027957001091

A Walk on the Wild Side –
Discover through the life of Jonah how you can partner with God, and see that He can be trusted even when we don't understand.
EAN: 5027957000964

Stop Looking for the Will of God –
Stop trying to find out what God wants you to do, and start seeking Him instead!
EAN: 5027957000957

£16.99 each (plus p&p)
Extra personal booklets: £2.50 each (plus p&p)

Singing in the Rain –
Examine the last seven days of Jesus' life, as seen through Mark's Gospel, and learn from His example how to deal with life under pressure. This six-session resource is ideal as a Lent study.
EAN: 5027957001183

£18.99 each (plus p&p)
Extra personal booklets: £3.50 each (plus p&p)

Prices correct at time of printing.

ELIJAH – PROPHET AT A LOSS

In *Elijah – Prophet at a Loss*, Jeff Lucas takes a look at the challenges Elijah faced in his walk with God and the lessons we can learn from him today.

For use in conjunction with the four-session DVD, *Life Journeys: Elijah – Prophet at a Loss*, this booklet includes questions for group discussion and four weeks of Bible reading notes by Jeff Lucas.

£2.50

LJDVDEJ

INDIVIDUAL AND GROUP
BIBLE STUDY GUIDES

www.cwr.org.uk

ISBN 978-1-85345-467-7

9 781853 454677

Tel: 01252 784700
Email: mail@cwr.org.uk

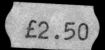

CWR Applying God's Word
to everyday life and relationships